LAST POST AND REVEILLE

Patrick Gordon-Duff-Pennington

with original drawings by
Alasdair McMorrine

HAYLOFT PUBLISHING LTD
CUMBRIA

First published by Hayloft 2014

Hayloft Publishing Ltd, South Stainmore,
Kirkby Stephen, Cumbria, CA17 4DJ

tel: 017683 41568
email: books@hayloft.eu
web: www.hayloft.eu

ISBN 978 190 452 4960

CIP data for this title are available from the British Library

Designed, printed and bound in the EU

Papers used by Hayloft are natural, recyclable products made from
wood grown in sustainable forest. The manufacturing processes
conform to the environmental regulations of the country of origin.

The dedication of this book is a long litany of thanks to Canon James Baker – a fellow revolutionary, his wife Anne lately Vicar of Muncaster and the Churches of Eskdale, and Alison Newcome, long suffering spouse of the Bishop of Carlisle.

For my parents, my teachers and family and for the people who have loved me and cared for me and taught me through all of my 84 years; for those who have led me in my blindness to wonderful places in hills and islands which most people are never lucky enough to see. They taught me to speak out without fear on behalf of those less privileged than me. Many of them had so little but took me into their homes and gave so much. To Hector Monro, Alick Buchanan-Smith, Russell Johnston and George Younger who fought so hard on behalf of common sense against philosophies of a theocratic government in the 1980s and 90s. For John McFall who came to me as a student from the Industry and Parliament Trust and became Chairman of the Treasury Select Committee. For Kenneth Mackenzie, Sam Mitha, and so many others in the Civil Service who became my friends and taught me discretion – if not respect – in dealing with the guardians of the public morals, even though the ethics of their posts gagged them.

Thanks are also due to Eric Robson who published my first two books, Isabel Fraser of the BBC, and Fordyce Maxwell of the 'Scotsman'. To Jo Wagstaff and

Sarah Knowles who translated my illegible writing into a legible text and above all to Dawn Robertson of Hayloft Publishing who published these poems at a time when it is very difficult to find a publisher to produce the work of a little known writer. Finally to Alasdair McMorrine my friend, who made the illustrations and the drawing for the cover.

Patrick of the Hills, 2014

CONTENTS

Last Post and Reveille	7
Lost	10
Widower's Lament	11
From Ulverston Station	12
My One	13
Cowal - time to go!	14
Face to Face	16
Grandmothers	17
For all things New	19
For Kazunori, Chieka, Maiko and Genta	21
Below the Falls of Pattack	22
Spöken for Berit	24
Sutherland Sky	27
Grief	28
Light of my Life	30
Meryll the Sculptress	31
Stately Home	32
For MVH	34
At Mains of Murthly	35
Anarchy – Agriculture at the Crossroads	36
An Eternal Question	38
A Wish	39
Simple Simon	40
Lonely Continent	42
Life	43
The End of the World	44
The Navigator	45
Night without a Moon	46
My Father's Plaid	47
Leaving Couldoran	50
Day of a Hundred Thousand Memories	53
Autumn	66
Forty Years On	67

Lord of all Hopefulness	69
The Gopher	70
Leaving Loch Laggan	71
Too Late for the Last Train	74
Dream on a Windy Night	76
Robin McCall – In memoriam	78
The Editor, 1993	80
Night	82
Lord Migdale's Daughter	83
A Reluctant Prisoner	85
This is my Destiny	86
Sunlight on the Sea	88
Milton with Meredyth	89
On Ben Alder at Night	91
For Solveig	92
Bloody House!	94
Laggan	95
Night after Night	97
A Whisper of Wind	98
Without You	99
At the Wishing Well	100
From Lismore	102
Requiem	104
In the Peer's Lobby, House of Lords	106
The Dark Mile	107
For the People of the Kholkhoz	109
Reflections on the Beshir Moons	111
Death Throes of an Old World	114
Reminder of the Grail	117
Grace à Dieu	118
In the Pentland Hills, 1952	119
Agnostics at Prayer	120
I'm Always There	121
September Trees	122
At Evening	123

LAST POST AND REVEILLE

I try to forget.
At best I am no more
Than a tinker in tatty clothes
Who travels up and down the roads of life
Talking to people in the ditches
When passing by. Remembering
All those who fed and sheltered me
Between the Hebrides and Edinburgh,
Shetland and Orkney, and Sutherland and the
                                        friends
I made from further south, recalling all those
                                        years
Of fighting for the people of the northern hills
Learning to be unafraid to challenge those
In powerful places and in government.

Now I am nothing, for my wife
Of six and fifty years is dead.
Unworthy as I was
She loved me and cared for me all that time,
Propping up the monstrous irrelevance
Of a too large house
Ingrained within her natal bones;
Rearing our four daughters and eight grand-
                                        children
Charming the unsuspecting visitors
Who shared our lives,

...continues

Standing at the front door in all her modesty
Pretending that she wasn't who she was,
Now the place feels empty. The final rites
Were said with due decorum.
I've done my best to help her
Dream her dreams of how the world should be,
But now she's gone, her ashes spread to the wind
Loved by everyone, but always unable to hear
The island songs which ring within my ears.
So now I am lonely
Not believing in any after life
Except for the genes we left
Within our children's children's blood
Knowing only that I want so much and need
A hand reached out across the sheets at night
To touch me as the stars
Shine down through moonlit window panes
Upon my sleepless head.
It's no disloyalty, but I must keep
Moving my limbs around my restless days,
Seeking some consolation for my inborn gifts
Of loving and giving, to someone else
Who needs them just as much as my dead wife.
I need some friend to come in their own right
And reach their hand across the empty bed
To reassure me that my world is not quite ended yet
And to listen to the wind together
Sighing in the trees, watching the clouds
Sweeping across the night time sky
Knowing I have another life to live
And someone else for whom to care
Until such time has come to go
Out of this careless world.

LOST

I search in the hills;
I search in the woods;
I search in the garden;
I search by the sea.
I search all the time
For a meaning of life –
And for you, and for me!
I search through old songs,
And I search in books;
I listen to music,
And look at old paintings –
Wherever I go I search
For my reason for life –
And for you, and for me!
And wherever I go,
In the hills, by the sea,
In the woods, in the garden,
I find – only you, only you
And my need for you here.
And the flow of your blood;
Through the flow of my blood;
And the sound of your words
In the words of my voice,
Are all that I have
Through the days and the nights,
When I am not there,
And you are not here –
By my longing side.
So I search all the time
For my reason for life –
And for you – and for me.

WIDOWER'S LAMENT

Too old to learn to love again, my sweet,
But only just, and yesterday,
Walking along in all that sudden summer sun
With crowds of happy people round about us,
It didn't seem impossible, so I shall quiver
At the thought of you beside me
Within the velvet darkness of tonight,
Your hand in mine, and I,
Waking to look into your eyes
At dawn, hoping some day
We two shall meet again.
Let it be soon!

FEOM ULVERSTON STATION

How many times
Must I still watch the agony of spring
Without you here –
The Ulpha fields grown green
Beneath the snow-topped hills that guard
The ageless valleys full
Of lambing ewes?

How many times have I to watch
The sun slip down
Beyond the silent sea
And know your hand reach out for mine
Across the night, and think I hear
Your voice
Call out to me?

How many times?

How many times have I to wish,
With you not here,
The distance dwindle into nothingness,
Hearing the echoes of a passing train
Across the darkened countryside?

In spring, I need you close to hold my hand –
With me, each night,
To watch the woodcock's mating flight.
I cannot bear this beauty of the bursting buds
Without you here, to tell
The music that my heart would share
With you until the end of time.

My One

You are the great loveliness in my life
Without whom I cannot live.
Today I have to go on a long journey.
If anything should happen to me,
Don't worry.
I'll meet you on the other side of the hills.
I want you to know,
Even beyond the bounds of time.
You will always be this total enchantment for me.
Having drunk with you from the same glass
I can never contemplate
Living without you –
Not now, nor ever –
You, who are the great loveliness
Of my whole life.

COWAL – TIME TO GO!

I came to Ardlamont
To gaze at the wide beyond
On an April day
With Arran smothered in clouds
And the driving mist
Just starting to lift in the south west wind.
I came to a place
That was filled with riddles for me.
How did a woman of Russian and Irish
And German and English descent
Come with her artist's eye
To live in the faraway place
With a room that felt filled
With the greens and the blues of the sea?
How did she look so young
With the grace of her well-held carriage
When I know for a fact
She was living her eighth decade?
What on earth did her two sons do
One of them, once an Oxford boxing blue.
And why had the land been let to MacRaes
On a stupid lease?
It felt to me like a place
Where the inmates were waiting to go
Over the waves to heaven.

And I thought of the Gaelic song
About the swans who returned
At the evening time to Cala.
So the place and the people
Just underlined
The thought in my mind that I, too,
Was awaiting to go quite soon
Out of the world as well
Across the waves in the picture that hung
Over the mantelpiece.
That's what I thought as I sat
In that seascape reflected room
On the innermost edge
Of the waiting sea.

FACE TO FACE

I sat in the chair this morning quite relaxed
In the corner of my dressing room
Face to face with Death.
"You come with me," the lady said
And thus it crossed my mind
How simple it might be
To slip away in quiet oblivion
Manacled to her, but life
Is not so easy and I had to stay
Pulling on my socks, wondering what
The point of living still might be,
Lingering on an endless road
To God knows where,
Oft terrorised by endless pain
And knowing all too well
It's still a long hard furrow that I have to plough
To reach my resting place and home
Beyond this tiresome day

GRANDMOTHERS

Grandmothers are special.
My grandfathers are dead –
The other grandmother too
And all that is left is my sister's
God-grandfather and you,
My own completely special grandmother
Who takes me for walks in the wood
And makes up stories about the crocodiles
Lurking in the ditches waiting to eat us up
And plays pooh-sticks with me
As we watch the fallen leaves
Swirling in the flow of the burn
They remind her of the time
She met my grandfather,
She, little more than a young girl
In the Wrens, from south west England
And he, a young army officer
Passing through London in the War.
She is quite famous now,
Author of numerous books,
And still so modest that she would be
Reluctant to admit to even being
Her grand-daughter's grandmother.
As we watch the leaves
Eddying around the mythical crocodile's nose
On their way to a mythical sea

...continues

A romantic poem I remember comes to my head
and makes me love my grandmother even more
Thinking of her partnership with her husband.
It went like this
'Not any more
Can I resist you in my life...
This is my destiny'
So, my beloved grandmother
Know that the stories we made up together
In the golden autumn woods
Will never be forgotten.
For me there's little doubt
We'll meet again in Heaven,
But in the meantime let us float
A few more sticks
Under the collapsing bridge
And know you are what any child would want
Their grandmother to be.

FOR ALL THINGS NEW

You stand
For all things new –
A hope of spring
To follow winter days,
With the beauty of daffodil trumpets
After the snow.

I find in you
All that I mind about –
The mist covered mountains waiting
For the return of the curlews
While they stand, listening to the
                    wind in the trees below,
And the rushing through the rocks of waters
Swollen by melting ice.

You are.
All of that cleanliness I left behind
With the innocence of the childhood days
When I used to walk back with my
                    sweets from the shop
Through the Morayshire fields,
Where they stood before harvest time
Studded with blue chicory and the red
Of the scarlet poppies
Among the swelling ears
Of the ripening oats.

For the learning I found
At Eton in the War,
And afterwards at Trinity, Oxford,

...*continues*

For all the knowledge of the beauty of music
That my mother taught me,
For those you stand, as well;
Just as much as for the feelings of a young officer
On a parade ground in the Carinthian hills,
Dipping the Regimental Colour in a Royal Salute,
Remembering his childhood countryside,
Still ignorant of a sweetheart waiting
And the unopened bud.
For the shepherd at the lambing
Under the Northern Lights
And the attendance on a Shorthorn cow
At midnight in the byre,
When it lay tied
Straining with rhythm while we eased the calf
On to the straw.
For the brairding of the May turnip seed
In the rigged up drills in the glens
And the greening once more in June
Of the upland pastures.
For the bloom of the machair flowers,
And the surge of the summer sea
In the innocent isles:
For the merciless speed,
And the grace of the scimitar set
Of a peregrine's wings
At the kill of a grouse.
For all of those you stand,
You, who found me, so little ago,
Gazing, exhausted, over a garden gate.
Now it is spring, and you are all to me,
I have told you, you stand – for life!

FOR KAZUNORI AND CHIEKA TSUJIKAWA,
MAIKO AND GENTA

Before you came
We never really knew
Anybody else from Japan.
You brought us the gift of your country
In your eyes,
And in the way you smiled,
So now it is time for you to go
My heart is full of tears.
Always the memory will stay
Of the delicacy of your thoughts
Like a branch of blossom
Across my window in spring.
I shall think that thought
Whenever I watch these hills
I watched so short a time ago
With you beside me
In the evening sun.

BELOW THE FALLS OF PATTACK

You are the pool of stillness
That I seek so desperately
To discipline the wildness
Of my daily life
With all the hither and thither
Of its frantic swinging
To and fro
From north to south,
To east to west.
I have no peace,
Seeking for something that I know,
Deep in my heart,
I'm destined not to find.
So when at night
Before I sleep
I find your gentleness
Tingeing my thoughts,
It is with gratitude
I recognise your stillness
As the drug I need so much
To calm the fury of my hectic life
And let me dream.

Spöken for Berit

I shall never forget the evening
I fell in love with you,
Old man and child we were,
By the foot bridge
Over Akerselva.
Do you remember, too,
How we walked down between the houses
From the home of our friends
To the place where the river runs
Beneath the old factory building,
With the ghosts of the girls
Who used to work
Making the clothes?
Old Rudolf Nilssen's ghost,
And Oskar Braathen's ghost
They both still watch,
But now they cannot write
The poem that I need for you.
My heart is full of tears.
You came so late to my life
With all the light
Of the western valleys
Still in your dancing eyes.
Now I must go – too soon –
But meeting you was for me
Like standing under the curtains of fire
Across the Arctic sky
On winter nights.

Perhaps we shall meet again,
But if we should not, next year
When the blossom comes to the trees in May
Try to remember the way that it was
In those special moments
Caught up from time,
Like the leaves of autumn
In the hands of children.

When you are married,
With children all of your own,
And the care of a loving man,
I hope you will never forget
That one such incredible moment of life
When we stood on the bridge –
I old, you young,
And our thoughts were entwined.

The tenderness there on the air between us
Was more, then, I think
Than most of the rest of the world
Can ever have
In the whole of their lives.
That's how it was for me –
And I guessed a little for you –
With the moon shining down
On the roofs of the houses
Beside the bridge over Akerselva,
This year in October
When you went away
Into the dark of the autumn night.

...continues

Perhaps I shall never be lucky
Nor meet you ever again,
But take me just once,
If only inside your mind,
To the valleys near Trondheim
When the flowers come out once more
Some spring.

That was the thought that I had
While Rudolf Nilssen's ghost,
And Oskar Braathen's ghost
Watched where we stood on the bridge
By Akerselva as the stars came out
And you kissed me goodbye
Last night.

SUTHERLAND SKY

If you weren't there
Where would I be
With no belief in God,
Or government, or me?
No place to put my thoughts
And visions
As I wander through the countryside
Or listen to the waves
Beside the evening sea.

Were you not there
My ear could hear no sound
And there would be
No place to yearn for
In the lonely dawn;
Robin would have no space
To drop his notes
Sitting among the branches
Of the weeping pear.

My heart would have no beat,
And I no quickening pulse
To hear the calling of the wind
Among the autumn grass
When stalking deer.
I could not bear to watch
The silver water under sky
While greylag geese return –
Without you there.

GRIEF

I can't reach you today.
Can't see your face.
Nor hear the lilt of your dear voice,
Even down the distant telephone wires.

So now
I suppose I shall never wake
Up in your arms again
And hear the robin sing
Songs under our bedroom window;

Never –
Fall asleep beside you
At peace
In our own bed,
Listening to the wind
And the tide running in the Island sounds.

Never –
Walk in the hills,
And spy the deer,
And hear the foxes call:
See snowdrifts pile
Against the forest fence.

Nor lie together by the mountain burns
Watching the trout
Flicking their tails
Among grey stones
In crystal pools.

For all that "Thou art my waking,
Thou my dreaming",
For ever and always,
In this distant place of exile
So far from the home hills.

The garden is dead this morning
With no birds singing
Here at Muncaster.
I am a prisoner.
You are gone!

LIGHT OF MY LIFE

You are all I have
The peace of sunlit hills
And noise of wind at war among the tossing trees;
Echoes in caves,
And waves
Lapping on lonely shores

And you are all the sympathy
I ever had for anything –
For people suffering, or dogs in need,
And ewes I helped
Licking astonished lambs
In April fields

You are for me the gentleness
Of holding pulse of goldcrest's heart beneath my
                                        hand
After it stunned itself
Against a branch,
And then watching it fly away
Into a waiting larch.

Oh! You are love and friend to me,
Are everything I have;
Without you now,
And all the music that you bring to me,
There would be nothing left
Worth breath.
My life is yours.

MERYLL THE SCULPTRESS
for Meryll Evans

One winter dawn, quite soon,
I'll come at last
Out of a wide unknown
With battered wings
To sit awhile
Under the calm authority
Of your unruffled hands,
Needing so much to find
A little space until,
At one week's end,
I'll have to leave once more
The quietness of the resting place
And once more face
The turbulent uncertainty
Outside.

This house
Is an enormous liability,
But it is a warm and friendly place
Where dogs are allowed to sit
In the chairs
Of an afternoon –
And people are welcome.
It is of use
To the local community
As a focus
For all their troubles and their needs
Which have to be announced
In quite explicit terms
To men who make the laws
Three hundred miles away
In Parliament.
Without a stand like that
The place is quite irrelevant.
Although time was
Not long ago
It was no more
Than some dead enclave
Of isolated privilege
Quite unrelated to the needs
Of a native population
In a decaying countryside.
Those days are behind us now
People are kind
And in concern for me may say
"Why do you take
Such awful punishment,

Mental, financial, physical,
Each day's strain,
Knowing quite well
In ten years' time your family
May not be here?"
I look at it
A little differently
Knowing I have to do my best
To leave behind the place
As an asset,
After I've gone,
For all the people
Of West Cumberland.
So I plant trees,
And mend the roof
For some far generation
Who may not even be
My children, but I know,
Though people laugh,
That this is the one quite valid thought
Which makes
Life in this place
Not quite impossible,
And almost worth
The awful effort
That is killing all around.
If fight I must,
Let me at least
Fight with a smile upon my face
And a light in my eyes,
Knowing that what I am thinking
Is what I believe to be right.
That is the meaning of this house.

For MVH

Came to the House of the Black Rock
Again last night
At evening time –
Campanulas and geraniums
In the kitchen window, and outside
The sun on the evening heather.
Beside us, in the garden.
Full of the spirit
Of my friend who made it,
Eucryphias stood
Wide-open-eyed above the house,
And the pyrus salicifolia
Weeping uncontrolled
For the Argyll that time has destroyed.
We walked to the top of the hill
With the dog,
Hearts full of lament for the changing land
And the greed of men.
We took our salt and sat by the fire
Full of the memories
Of that first rainswept night
When I came to the House of the Black Rock.
Today I go, out of a long ago,
Back to my private wars,
Full of the untold sadness at leaving the place
But at peace, looking forward to the time
Of the next meeting place.

At Mains of Murthly

This is quite ridiculous –
Even here, perched high above the Tay
At Aberfeldy, I find it quite impossible
To escape your shadow,
But am so glad the way, quite suddenly,
You came a part of my old life
Amidst these hills where first I worked.
Among the Blackface sheep
In a place intensely beautiful,
Through endless bitter winter weeks
Working the saw outside the Ruskich door,
Lighting the lamp to put the hens to bed,
When snow dictated what work we undertook
And sent us day after day
So tired to bed – too tired to dream
Even of you in a far off place.
You took one road and I another
Quite unsuspecting that sometime far away
Our lives might accidently coincide,
A strange collision of two awaiting minds.
We've had our lives, our families,
Our partners passed away.
We did not ask for this,
I thought my life was done
But then you came.

ANARCHY – AGRICULTURE AT THE CROSSROADS

"Abolish science" the wise ones said,
Wrapped in an urban cocoon,
"Outlaw the chemical sprays," they said,
And half of us half believed it true,
But man seeks the balance
None can achieve
Twixt well-filled stomach
And easy mind.

Where have they gone?
I was starting to ask,
Poppy and scarlet pimpernel,
And chicory's waving blue,
Which used to pervade our childhood,
Now missing these many years
From the rows of the ripening grain
In the limitless "weed-free" fields.

But all of a sudden, and one by one,
Out of the maiden earth,
Coaxed by the urban naturalist,
They've had a triumphant rebirth;
And one by one as the combines
Are silenced by lack of oil,
Our children's children may have to go back
To coaxing reluctant prickles
From fingers at harvest time
As the weed seeds spring from the fertile soil

And man returns to an ancient toil.
And those who may still remember
Will weep tears for the unsprayed acres
Of their newly neglected land.
As they curse the return of the thistle,
While extracting reluctant prickles
From the cracks of reluctant hands.

But man still seeks balance
That none can achieve
Twixt well filled stomach
And easy mind.

An Eternal Question

The sun swipes down
In torrid unaccustomed heat
Out of a molten sky.
My eyes are tired, and red,
Looking for you, and never finding you
Who seem so much too far away.
People are sad and worried everywhere;
The restless clouds of war,
And terrible starvation mass
Over the weeping world,
Just as the blackness of rain,
Brooding over the fells at the top of the valley.

People are sad and worried everywhere
And the too many do not understand.
Not enough money; not enough time;
Women grieving for dead partners;
Children who will never return;
And all of us searching in vain for the
                                            meaning of life.
How can there be a God, we ask?

It must be a time, I suppose,
For eyes to glance down in the field,
And to push the reluctant hoe
Through the weed-ridden drills
Of the turnip field.
A week to work.......
But where are we going – we ask?

A WISH

Over to the west lies the sea of my longing
Lapping silver in the moonlight around the shores
Of the Isles.
I want nothing but the peace of those places
And the chant of the monks in the abbey
Of Iona.
I see in my mind the evening sun setting over the
                              Treshnish Isles
Beyond the Sound of Ulva
With Bac Mhor lying in the evening sea
Along with its sad memory
Of the girl with her nursing child
Left alone to die when her man was lost
Never to return
From the fishful water towards Tiree
And I, I am anchored to the mainland
Unable to move my shackled limbs
From the ties of the heaps of stones
And money, and land, and law
Yet still in my dreams I hear
The seabirds cry and the call of the sea
Far to the West ready to take me home
To my resting place.
"I want no easy grave" some Irish poet wrote.
The same for me. Only a place
Where I can forget, and be forgotten
Untied from my frail mortality.

Simple Simon

I need a home –
I've had a place,
But I need a home
With someone in it
Who loves me,
And whom I can love

I do not need
Wealth or possessions,
But I want so badly
To live somewhere
Where I
Am more important
Than the accumulated goods
Of centuries –
Not just
A part of the heritage
Part of the castle walls.

Life has more to it
Than that,
More than being
Just another of the stags' heads
In the hall.
Life is for living,
But in this place
We are dead.

Dead from exhaustion,
From trying to prop up
Four fifths of a thousand years,
Which have sucked the blood
From a family
And those who have served
In this miserable place.

I need to go home
To a place
Which has some future
With someone in it to share
Not just possessions,
But thoughts and ideas;
Who knows how to give
With their mind
As well as their heart –
Not living their life
In retrospect –

I do not desire
A house or residence,
As some sort of symbol of state
Which is turned to a gilded cage;
Just a small place
Is all that I need
With auricula plants in the garden
And a house
With rooms that are
Sunny and warm.

LONELY CONTINENT

What use
Are all those lovely things that live
Within the prison of my life
If you're not there
To share with me
This beauty that I find
Is everywhere.
I need you all the time.
And want you too.
I've learnt through you
To be, perhaps, too sensitive
But God! How beautiful I find the world
Because you're here – alive –
Upon this lonely continent
Knowing as well as I
This life we share.

LIFE

As waves
Around the Western Isles,
And like my tartan is,
The whole of my small self
Is woven round you now,
And each of us
Just marking time
Until the stepping stone
That's next –
A constant changing miracle
Of you and I –
And us –
Among the brilliant chaos
Of our tangled lives.

THE END OF THE WORLD

When the world has ended
And the last stars have burned away
When there are no more promises
And no more dawns;
When the last lark song has vanished
Down the aisles of the absent years
And the wild seas have spilt
Through the base of the earth
Somewhere within that silent nothingness
There will be light
Still fired from all the blended thoughts
Of yesterday
And all the thousand smothered flames
Of you, in a faraway place,
And of me here
Among the midnight hills.

THE NAVIGATOR
for Chou Hayes

You are the anchor and the quiet bay
When all the world I know
Dashes about on journeys
Wondering why.
At evenings, after turbulence,
My ship needs steadying
And you are there
In a place I understand
And when you gently come,
Gliding insistent to my mind,
I feel the storm abate
About the madness of my life
And know I have a bay
To anchor in.

NIGHT WITHOUT A MOON

I'm all alone.
Nobody cares.
The realities of the people I once knew
Sound only as ghost echoes in my memory.
It is all right in daytime when I talk to people
passing by,
But travelling the darkened corridors of night
Means striving through an endless sea,
Climbing the glassy waves in cold numb misery,
Terribly afraid in a life without an end.

Sleeping, I dream only bad dreams.
I don't belong any more to any place, to anybody.
And I must swim for ever and ever
Without a hope of reaching back
To the far off shores of some reality.

I see no colours except grey and black,
No calm lagoon;
Everything hurts; worst of all
The blurred remembrance of the person I once was
In times when I mattered a little,
In the times when I minded what happened.
Now I don't mind, and don't matter to anybody,
And what I think and what I feel does not matter.
In so far as I pray, I pray only for the dull anaesthetic
Of forgetfulness

And the passing of life,
For I am all alone,
And nobody can reach me now,
Nobody cares.

My Father's Plaid

Seeing my kilts
Hanging in the cupboard
When I went up to bed last night,
I knew I wished so much to see you wear
My tartan;
Wanted to fold you in my father's plaid,
To give to you the pride I used to have.

I wore a kilt
From early childhood days.
The tartan brings back memories
Of dancing class, and nursery tea;
Of Sunday lunch with Duffy, and the aunts;
Of mince, and polished dining rooms,
And silver owls, with amber eyes,
And Madge, the maid;
Of eating bran in garden sheds,
The brown Leghorns,
The loganberries under nets.
I planted Dusty Millers in my own small patch.

And in my army days, Fort George.
We mounted guard, and once a week
The pipe band beat retreat.
I hear the *Battle of the Somme*
Across the ramparts still,
The drums, and drummer boys,
Whose hair must now be grey

...continues

Like mine,
Tapping their rhythm
By the evening firth.
My passing out parade at Eaton Hall.

Battalion slow march across the barrack square,
Among Carinthian hills;
Dip of the colours for a royal salute,
And all the men presenting arms.
Mackenzie 92 playing *The Mist Covered*

Mountains

Among the Dolomites at far Lienz,
Or marching back from exercise
Along the dusty Austrian roads.

Jocks singing: *I love a lassie,*
Crossing the flooded Lieser in the ice
And snow.
Evan Macrae, the pipe major
I had a kiss of the King's hand
Playing the pibroch in the candlelight,
His bearded shadow moving on the wall.

As junior subalterns we had to dance
The foursome reel upon the table in the Mess
When people came to dine.
I remember
All the army pipers
Marching into Parliament Square
On June 2nd., 1953.
The day we crowned the Queen.

All the blue bonnets are over the Border,
With the marvellous tune sweeping among
The high buildings
Away into the sky.

Later, I always wore my kilt:
Sometimes, my dog with me,
Running away wide on the steep hillsides
When we went to the gatherings.

3am into the early morning hills,
So that the sheep travelled in the cool of the day.
I wore them when I crawled
Among September stags,
Or ploughed the field with bare cold knees
In spring.

And when I saw them hanging there
Last night.
It all seemed suddenly a growing-up for you,
Who are so like my tartan kilts,
A bold incitement to a hero's life.
And that is why, when we are old –
One day, some time – I long to see
My father's father's plaid
Around your shoulders in the fireside chair.
With me beside you reading books,
And you beside me telling tales,
Before we go to bed –
And sleep, and sleep, and sleep,
Resting together till the morning comes.

LEAVING COULDORAN

All night, last night, the gale
With men at meetings swapping lies
With limitless good nature
Sipping their whisky by the autumn fire
While the wild wind rattled the window panes
Outside.
Was it only yesterday,
Away from the door of Couldoran
Of the great sadness
With the pony boy drowned
In the floods of the previous night.

Away from the arms of shelter
Out of the caring of my friends
I had to go into a wider world.
Sunshine and shadow as I crossed
September hills past Attadale
Over the pass,
Into the foot of Glen Shiel
Where the rock skirts of the Sisters
Were white with the frantic foaming
Of the sudden autumn spate.

Farewell to Couldoran of the grieving burns.
Farewell for a while to my friends,
Mark on his way to Inverness,
Gillian and Jennifer, waving at the door.
Arriving at Iain Campbell's house.
He was sitting beside his fire,
Waiting to stalk, but the furious day

Too angry for killing deer.
Over the Minch to Harris
On the afternoon boat
From Uig in Skye
To a Deer Group meeting
At the Tarbert Hotel.
No hinds being killed at Eishken now.
A grave error by an absent owner.
When morning came we drove
Along the corrie foot
At Ahmunnsuidhe through the shafts
Of sunlight on the green and sodden hills
Where the dun deer watched us
In their shelter from the storm.
To Huisnish beach, then back
To Uist on the midday boat.
Past South Harris in the lea of a shore
Unshocked by the fierce gales
On the western side of the Isles.
Lochmaddy to Askernish and back,

But through it all my mind was full
Of my friends by their generous hearth
At Couldoran.
Glad I was that I came to the West
On the day that I did
To be able to place my hands in theirs
And, just for a very short time,
To share the shock
Of their awful sadness.

...continues

Gone away through the storms,
I discovered I knew I was leaving
The caring of a terribly special place
Where I would always find
A shelter stone in time of need.

So farewell for a little, my friends,
And farewell to Couldoran.
You could never have known when I came,
You and Couldoran it was
Who healed the impossible scars
Of another tearful goodbye
That I'd had to take that dawn.
I would wish, as I turn my money.
Tonight to the stormy moon
That soon we may meet again
Under a quieter sky.

DAY OF A HUNDRED THOUSAND MEMORIES

Yesterday we went back to Ospisdale again
To see Margaret, six hundred and four years,
Almost to the day, since they brought her
Namesake home, dead on the boat, to Embo.
Sutherland was beautiful, lost in the summertimes
Of the countless years between.
Long, long ago I studied history
But only now I start to understand
The long perspective of the Highland scene.
I did not realise how all the emotions
Of a simple life – all the experience,
All the happiness, all the tears
Could be drawn together into
A sudden clarity of understanding –
That is what you have done.
I started to see my life like a drowning man,
Remembering.
As a boy I lived in Moray
Near the edge of Findhorn Bay at Moy
At night my sister and I would hide
Behind the drawing room curtains with our
                              grandmother,
White-wigged watching
The great gold harvest moon
Light up the land outside.
We had our own garden, my three years younger
Sister and I,
Full of velvet auriculas, and columbine,
And purple and red anemones,

                                        ...continues

With violets and forget-me-nots, and polyanthus
Surrounded by a neat box hedge.
Willie, the under gardener, when nobody was looking
Let us crawl under the old fishing nets
To eat strawberries warm from the beds.
We had a nanny who spoilt us,
Taking us up to see her cousins at Wellhill
On still September afternoons.
We used to ride back home on Prince
From the evening fields. Clydesdales were important
Their ribbons and their harness at the shows
And the clack and jangle of the harrows
Across the springtime tilth
If we were good they let us collect
The brown eggs from the nesting boxes
And sometimes we were pecked trying to reach
Too eager hands under a clocking hen.
Once there was a constipated duck
Who had to be dosed with castor oil
Under the kitchen sink. It died!
And when Nannie was married to Alastair Shaw,
A farmer with hands like soup-plates
From Upper Slackbuie, near Inverness,
Her place was taken by Peggie
Who wasn't very nice, but she did have a boyfriend
Who had a motorbike, and drove us up and down
To the suspension bridge at the Broom of Moy.
One day with him we found a yellowhammer's nest
In the grass by the edge of the road,
Which somewhat justified the existence of Peggie.
There was an Alsatian called Sheba, who gave us rides,
And a piebald Shetland pony called Beauty, who didn't
Much. Sometimes in summer

We stayed with our grandmother, Duffy
At Hopeman Lodge, and ate loganberries and
                                    handfuls of bran
From the kist in the garden shed.
Duffy had budgerigars in the aviary outside
And a parrot which ate the backs of all the books.
There were silver owl pepper pots on the table
And rich brown eggs to eat. Perpetual smell
Of mince and pepper in the dining room
And, in a pinafore and black dress,
A maid called Madge. My sister
Threw an iron at me and split my head.
At night, from the window seat in the nursery,
Before we said our prayers, we used to watch
The fishing fleet with coloured sails
Slipping up the firth on the evening wind.
Occasionally a warship sailed out from the Cromarty
                                    Firth.

Morven of Caithness stood always there
A magical distant hill. Aunt Rat's Tails,
Called Margaret too, but known as Git,
Taught us to ride a bicycle.
She was reputedly the thinnest woman
In the north of Scotland
Her tummy meeting her backbone
Which caused her endless trouble.
Eventually she emigrated to a timber house
In Dorset where the woodpeckers
Caused pandemonium by pecking holes
In the roof. She did her weeding
Her wig perched on the fork beside her.

...continues

My father shot and fished six days a week
And trained dogs. I admired
His multicoloured fishing flies
And thought that catching salmon must be easy.
In 1936 he and my mother were divorced
She had the money and he was rather poor.
That year the other grandmother
Had the shooting at Trinafour
At the top of Glen Errochty
And I fell in the pool underneath the bridge
Below the post office, the day
My sister and I were told of the divorce.
Our mother and father married again,
We, the children, were shuttled from one to the other
And learnt to make the most of it.
I always screamed when I went back to school
Which wasn't fair, because parents and step-parents
Were all conscientiously kind
Even though they probably felt like braining us.
War came when I was nine years old.
My stepfather had rented a large house
On the top of Boxhill called Bellasis
Where we lived through the Battle of Britain
And the Blitz. It was a time of intense awareness
With planes and parachutes falling out of the sky
And at night a red inferno over London.
I saw a kingfisher for the very first time
On the day that Paris fell
Flitting through arcades of alders
Down a long dark river reach
Near Mickleham.
My second prep-school – I kicked up such a fuss

...continues

At the first, I was removed – was evacuated
From Seaford, first to Cornwall for a term,
Where I learnt the wildflowers.
The thrifts were very beautiful.
We collected cowries on the beach, under the cliffs,
While the guns fired at the German bombers
Over Falmouth.
After that to Devon, near
Where Henry Williamson wrote *Tarka the Otter.*
It was a paradise of birds at Castlehill.
Linnet's nest at the bottom of the garden,
Wren's nest in a bank near the bandstand
And a grey wagtail's nest
In the stones of Ogley Bridge
Buzzards circling high over Oxford Down
And ducks, and swans, and herons by the river.
I shared a small room in a dormitory
Called "Mind Your Head" with a boy named
Robin Hooper, godson to Dr. Garbett,
Archbishop of York. He swallowed a key
When he walked in his sleep.
The key came out with brown bread
But we never met again.
I yelled going back to school
Until I was sixteen.
At Eton in the war
We were taught by the most liberal men
And although we were living through one war
I think, in retrospect,
We lived much more in the shadow of the one before.
We learnt classics with Llewellyn Slingsby Bethell
Who made us translate the local paper
Into Latin and Greek verse – twenty lines of each

Each week.
And I read the whole of Rudyard Kipling under the desk
While the headmaster, Claude Aurelius Elliot,
Economist and mountaineer taught us Industrial
                                                        History,
We played games hard and lived
As though there was no tomorrow.
For some there wasn't.
Every Saturday night the names of old boys
Killed during the week
Were read out in College Chapel.
We still believed in Empire and the civilising influence
Of the British, lately revealed as a shameful sham.
I thought I wanted to go into the Colonial Office.
My stepfather fought in Burma
Commanding an East African anti-tank regiment,
And I learnt 'I want to go home' in Swahili.
We didn't like the Japanese.
My mother still doesn't, but I have charming friends,
Kazunori and Chieko Tsujikawa, and have featured
As centre-spread in Japanese *Playboy*
Dressed in an old overcoat fastened with twine
And slightly embarrassed in the middle of all the pages
Of beautiful ladies dressed in next-to-nothing at all!
My mother dosed herself with gin
And we played chess on the guard's van floor.
All the time I looked at the maps of the hills.
We caught fish at Lochnidorb on windy days,
I poached a partridge, and was caught.
Occasionally we saw deer, but I never had
Anyone or anything to whom I could relate
All the beautiful things that I saw.

...continues

It's still just as bad, which is, I suppose
Why I am writing this to you.
We always had the Ellises to stay
Or stayed with them at Dulnain Bridge.
Roger smoked cigarettes in the train – he now denies –
On our way back from our prep school.
We shared rooms at Oxford
Underneath the clock at Trinity.
The Grinling Gibbons mantelpiece
Is now considered much too good
For modern undergraduates.
We acted Shakespeare's plays for our mothers,
I was Macbeth!
Other times we did scenes from the Bible,
Hanging Roger's poor sister, Julia
From the drawing room door by her pigtails
As Absalom, my son!
She's now a famous skin specialist
My mother ran a YMCA canteen around North Wales,
Rented a house near Oswestry, where she kept
Chickens, and pigs, and bees, and we ran wild.
Up to Oxford in 1948
To Trinity to study Modern History,
But could never understand why it should begin in 55BC.
The only lectures attended
Were Alan Bullock on Hitler
And a man in the Indian Institute
Who had been a spy in Afghanistan
In 1919. He could have told
Tony Blair never to go anywhere near the place.
I hunted the beagles and spent
All of the summer term
With a rifle at Bisley where the nightingales

Sang in the dark.
I learnt to write backwards
And went to Ireland after Christmas
With Pierce Carrigan to hunt.
In retrospect I don't know why I did it,
But at the time, with snow on Slievenamon
And the Golden Vale below, life at Clonacody
Was special and completely mad,
Filled with beautiful horses, and snipe bogs
And unbelievable stories told by grooms
In a broad Irish brogue.
How I got a degree, I shall never know.
Once they threatened to rusticate me
For failing Historical Geography in my prelims,
But I found that Reggie Weaver, the President
Was keen on roses. With the aid
Of a book from the library
I learnt all about black spot and aphids.
My mother's inherited silver tongue
Finished the argument.
We learnt to live, but when I think
How little I know and how many people
Have good degrees like me,
I am quite certain half of them
Aren't worth the paper they are written on!
My results were totally unexpected.
Having answered a multiple choice question
'Describe the effects of the silting up
Of the River Scheldt on European History'
I was just as astonished as my inquisitors
To have got it right, and achieved a good 2nd.
The education we had in life

...*continues*

Testing hypotheses on our colleagues,
Learning not to lose our tempers in an argument,
Discovering the constant need for compromise,
Made us many friends from all around the world.
And when we left, we left
With a basic knowledge of the tides of history
And fairly open minds, too absent now
From the brains of current politicians
With narrow views and not much common sense.
They wish to rule us and do not realise that power
Is just a dangerous aphrodisiac.
I joined the army for my National Service.
It was a good summer at Fort George in 1951.
The day I joined we were given our jabs
For tetanus and typhoid.
They were very sore and in the night
Delirious Jocks from all around the Western Isles
Groaned in Gaelic in their misery
Never having been away from home before.
I had two books – *Mine Eyes unto the Hills*
And *Sparkenbroke*. Next day
We moved to the Potential Leaders hut.
The man in the next door bed, called Bremner
Was saving up to use the loo at home
In Forres on his Sunday leave, three weeks away
And became very ill. The man
On the other side was a coal miner
From Fife. He deserted.
The man beyond him painted pink ducks
On the barrack room walls and threw them bread.
He was sent away – mightily relieved.
The plugs from the bath had been stolen long ago
So we had to use socks.

It was a tough life and we became very fit.
To leave camp we had to stand over a mirror in the
                              guard room floor
For the orderly sergeant to ensure
We wore nothing under our kilts
Nor were we allowed on the top decks of buses
In case we offended the prim old ladies of Arderseir
On their way to Inverness.
The corporal in charge of us was called Maclean,
Formerly a butcher boy in Motherwell,
He was the finest leader I have ever met.
The cooks from the ATS washed their stockings
In the cooking pots and the food was terrible.
Those from homes far worse than mine
Refused to eat it. I could have eaten a horse.
Each day at evening the pipers beat retreat.
I can still hear the march,
The Battle of the Somme, ringing in my ears.
And very soon the unique privilege
Of being a Cameron Highlander was understood.
Six weeks of basic training ended quickly
And I often wonder what happened to my companions.
After six weeks, three or four of us were sent
To Barton Stacey for our Officer Selection Board
Where I gave my five minute lecturette
On the 'pleasures of being alone'
And in retrospect I am astonished
I was ever given a Commission.
After four weeks we left the Fort
And went to the OCTU at Eaton Hall
Where we paraded, endlessly paraded,

...continues

Under the watchful eye of Regimental Sergeant Major
Copp, Coldstream Guards.
We ran and jumped, flying through trees
In full battle order, worming underneath nets
On our bellies helping each other in teams of four
Over walls impossibly high,
Defying death and thoroughly enjoying it.
We marched for miles and miles.
We raced across the countryside,
Fired on the ranges at Sealand
And in the evening went to the cinema
In Chester where I always fell asleep.
Afterwards to Cunninghams's Oyster Bar.
We had lectures on hygiene and tactics,
More on religion.
We went to battle camp to Trawsfynnydd
And Okehampton, and traversed the middle of Wales
By night, by compass
Through limitless bogs, and awful snow.
After tea we polished our boots
Until we could see our faces in the toe caps.
We pressed our uniforms
Learning to remove the scorches
By rubbing with an old half-crown.
On St. Andrew's Day, 1951,
I spent an hour up to my waist
In a swollen river, with a Bren gun
At Trawsfynnydd, where at night
After we had dried our clothes,
I walked with a school teacher from South Wales

To see the statue of Hedd Wynn, killed on the day
Before he was due to return from the front in France
To receive the Bardic Crown. It was
An indelible memory, with the clouds
Flying across the moon,
And the wind in the telephone wires
And the statue of the man
Standing against the moonlit sky.
I passed out as Senior Under Officer
Taking the parade of nigh on a thousand men
On a March day in 1952.
The band of the Worcestershire Regiment
Couldn't play *Pibroch of Donuil Dhu*,
The Cameron march past
So we had to make do with *Hielan Laddie*.
I was dangerously proud.
In my ears there is still the echo
Of Sergeant Pile's staccato voice
'Pick up your bloody feet – sah'
And so I became 'Sir'
A young officer who knew it all –
And nothing!

AUTUMN

Can people see in my eyes
The reflection of you
That I know lies there?
Can they hear in my voice
The lilt of the words
I remember you speaking?

Do they know, when I look
That I look with your look,
And speak when I speak
With the words that you taught me to say,
That I caught from your caring?

Do they guess what I feel?
Do they know that my eyes,
And my voice, and my hands
Have been washed
With a touch of your loving?

Is it, I wonder,
A God-given gift that I pass to the world,
Or do I betray
Through the looks and the words,
The gigantic chasm of emptiness
Felt since your going?

FORTY YEARS ON.....

Last night you marched across my mind
With regiments of memories
Asking me how and why we'd gone,
Tramping the paths we trudged along
Marching God only knows to where.
You I remember very well –
We called you Iron Dominion then,
Those countless, countless moons ago,
Which was a poor repayment for
All the kindness that you showed
To everyone along your road.

Do you remember how we sat
And ate our lunch upon the hill,
With you beside the Crooked Man.
And he beside his crooked gun,
Those far off days of young September?

We listened to the wind sweep through
The myrtle bushes in the bogs.
Now, having no faith
I find it hard
To whistle and sing along rough paths
That lead in the end one wonders where,
And half suspects not any where.

One day when you have gone to Heaven,
While I am playing with fire below,
Perhaps we'll meet again some time
Along the frontier which divides
The good that's you, the bad that's me,
Gone to the devil long ago
Despite the prayers of many friends,
And in September lunch again,
Stop wondering what life was for,
And just enjoy the autumn sun
Once more among the calling grouse
Long safe from my redundant gun,
Remembering when our life was fun.

LORD OF ALL HOPEFULNESS

I am even more thrilled
Than that far child
Starting on his journey through broken images
Of clouds on rippled water –
Going in search of fish

I am conscious of you –
All the time as a part of me,
Poised at the edge of the next world;
Hurry, darling!
Many moons from now perhaps
We shall be making home
But for now, for us both, I think I know,
Like you,
Our journey should be a time of happiness –
Not waste.

THE GOPHER
for Lucy Bond

Ambleside Bus Station Enquiry

Sweet 21 – and a little bit more;
Beautifully dressed,
Undoubtedly bored,
She fetched and she carried,
For day after day,
The system's demands
To the Methodist Hall;
But when I am old
I shall always remember
The sweet wide smile
She gave to us all –
A flower bud in spring
As she dropped in her mouth
Her chocolate drops
In the Methodist Hall.

LEAVING LOCH LAGGAN

Will it be there
That I must find my destiny
Among those crowded city streets
Where men no longer smile,
Learning their lust for gold?
Or here –
Where in my youth I lambed the ewes,
Finding the harmony of wind, and sky, and hills?

Should it be there –
Among those cultures of an alien race,
Where men forget the poems of the Island seas,
And sunset on the silver sand –
Should it be there I am condemned to die
I would fear death,
But here,
Among these timeless Highland hills
I learned to love so long ago,
My hair brushed by the breeze,
My eyes alight with sky.
This is the Scotland that my fathers fought to keep
For which I, too, am quite prepared to die.

...continues

If I could have a single wish,
It is to lie eventually among the tartan moss
Where first I crawled,
Under the shadow of the eagle's wings,
Through herds of autumn deer,
Watching the woods below
The banks of yellow tormentil.
There I would wish to stay
At rest
Above the diamond waters of the sleeping loch,
Nursed by the memory
Of all the people who have taught me how to love
this place

As part of me, as part of life,
Far and away beyond
All greed for gold.

For this is home, and these,
These are the people and the land for which I fight
And here among these hills
For them
I would not be afraid to die.

Too Late for the Last Train

Woman, who came too late,
I cannot give you – though I would –
All of the gifts which have become
So long ago
No longer in my gift.
Too late in my life's history now
To hand you all my manhood,
Which you know I wished I could,
Wrapping you up at night
Within the cradle of my caring arms.
Too late to whisper now the comfort of endearing
words
Among the velvet darkness of tonight,
While equinoctial gales rampage around
Outside the peaceful house.
Too late, too late, to wrap you up,
To feel the pulse of your ecstatic heart
Against the beat of mine,
Watching the moonlit sea below the cliffs
When we wake up at night
But still, it was true, wasn't it,
As we walked through the arches of the autumn
trees,

You know how much I longed to pick
The ripe red apples from the sagging boughs.
There's something strange, I think,
Hanging upon the air between us both.
I only hope that we can learn to play it right
For our remaining days.
Now that I know I love you
Teach me the wisdom to build out of it
Something quite totally special, something quite
                                    different,
Something
Only for you.

DREAM ON A WINDY NIGHT
For Lucy Carrigan the most charming god-daughter

Sure, girlie, if this isn't ridiculous!
Why, if I were thirty years younger
I'd swoop down on Ireland like an eagle
And spirit you away
Across the Golden Vale
On the back of one of your father's yearlings;
But I'm not fit for the trembles like that,
Me, at my age –
Though I'm sure you'd get another medal
From the President
For community service
Keeping the old dodder going –
Me, not him!
I can just see your mother, though,
Beautifully brought up she was,
Nice woman she is,
Standing at the drawing room door
Saying "Oh dear!"
And your father, in the Room of Beautiful
                           Thoughts,
At least that's what it was called
Forty years ago,
With the picture of Jane Donoughmore on the
                           desk.
I often wonder if it's still there.

Well, father, he would be furious,
Not because his slip of a daughter
Had been stolen away by an old sugar daddy,
But because the brazen pair
Had ridden off into the clouds
On the back of his best yearling
Which he had just prepared for sale.
And, sure, I tell you what, you,
Not all the tongues of all the gossips
In the whole of Co. Tipperary
Could keep up with themselves,
Trying to keep up with the horse
And the two of us.
Wow! Me an old dodder
With dreams like that!
Even the idea makes me smile.
Meet you on the other side.
Of Slievenamon
Huh!?

ROBIN MCCALL – IN MEMORIAM

I'm very much upset at this man dying –
He was so much a part of my life
And the life of all those who loved him
That even the thought of him no longer there
Is a weight on our will to live.
I see him still – the way that he always was
When first we met, and he taught me then
How to survive in a hostile world
Where the snow, drifted by the wind,
Mounted up the windows, and we shovelled for
days
And days to reach the road –
When the porridge simmered all night
For our breakfast and he and I
Would sit by the fire at Ruskich
Of an evening, both of us sound asleep
In our chairs while Peggie sat in between us
Doing her mending or darning our socks.
He taught me – eventually – how to back a tractor;
How to strain a fence;
How to sow fertilizer out of a sheet;
How to cut the logs and set the snares
For the endless rabbits who made their runs

Through the fences below the woods which were
                                                    filled
With primroses and violets in spring.
He taught me how to milk a cow
Or lamb a ewe – after a fashion.
He taught me – in my terrifying ignorance –
How to inject a lamb and dose a tup.
Above all he taught me how to swing
With the world as we climbed the hill
On our way to the gathering in the early morning;
And a thousand other things did this man teach me
I know that his family
Will feel a gaping hole in their everyday lives
And that I, like them, must learn
To still breathe fire.
The world turns yet and now, because of him
And the wisdom he taught to those whose life he
                                                    touched,
It is we who must learn to survive
In the places he taught us to love.

The Editor

He sits reporting faithfully
The little tragedies of local life –
The widow who'd been robbed
Of all her savings that she kept
Inside her dresser drawer;
The drunkard who had lost his job
Returning home to break the nose
Of someone who had tried
To steal his wife.

The unsuccessful local football team
The seagulls shitting in the street,
And factories closed at Lillyhall,
And the village shops and the post office.
And the unemployed
Stretching back in people's memories
To 1931.

Ennerdale Show and Gosforth Show
With the sons of the fathers featured there
As competitors thirty years ago,
Holding their winning tups
Or leading a Friesian cow,
And the dole queue
With people with nothing to do.
That man, he's done his best
Coming as he has from the land
Of the Jarrow March

To Whitehaven and Cleator Moor.
He's reported the work of the church,
And the Women's Institutes
And births, and deaths,
And Sellafield.
Our apathy has shaken him
As we wait for something to happen
Maybe tomorrow.

Today, moved by his plea
I wrote to the Prime Minister
And four of his colleagues
Telling them it was a peculiar way
To run a country when nobody seemed
Able to decide
Whether to open Thorp or not
And West Cumbria was crucified.

As I looked into the faces
Of the people worried about their jobs
I wanted to tell him
Sitting behind his Queen Street desk
That somebody somewhere
Had listened across the years
And knew what he meant when he'd said
Ordinary people like you and I must
Protest or as sure as fate
The world would forget and we,
At the end of our lonely twisted road,
For want of a word, would surely die.

NIGHT

I dread the night
For that, of all times,
Is the time I miss you most.

The clock strikes two,
Strikes three;
At four I tell myself
I must be sensible.
And try to sleep.
I listen to the news at five,
At six I rise,
Making my way
Along the silent corridors.

Outside, among the trees
The sodden darkness grips
My rasping throat.
Dogs bark at Waberthwaite.
A restless duck wakes up
Along the river bank.

I wander through the dripping woods,
Besieged by gloom,
Until at length
I meet another day
Behind the hills.
And so it is,
With you far off
And I, alone

LORD MIGDALE'S DAUGHTER

Dreamer of dreams,
Don't worry for I could not fall
In love again
With anyone, but you and Prickles
Are a distant certainty
Inside the rudeness of my life,
Some tiny compass point
By which to steer my ship
On nights like this
Between the narrow rocks
Of day by day,
When I go round and round
The edge of Scotland
Trying to make the Scottish
Country people feel
They're needed when
The Southern English seem to say
They're not.

The sight, within my mind,
Of you among your sheep this year
Has given back the thought
Of better days to me –
The sense of early morning
In the lambing field,
With larks singing before the dawn
And gentle hands
Sorting the complications

...continues

Of a twisted lamb
That is what life's about.
This is not, could not be,
A calling or a coming home
The way you feared
For me;
Only a distant cry of gratitude
For you – and Prickles –
And the dreaming that you have
So far away
Across the miles of storm tossed night
Which seem to be
The rotten story of my life
These days.

A RELUCTANT PRISONER

I know
How animals in cages feel,
For not so long ago
I walked the mountain tops
And felt my legs swing free
Across the summer grass,
But now I'm here at Muncaster,
Imprisoned in a gilded cage by circumstance.
I've lost my freedom, lost my hope,
And never more may know
The sun upon my moving limbs,
The music of the wind among the rocks;
So now I understand how lions feel
In cages.

This is my Destiny

Not any more
Can I resist you in my life
You the swirling torrent, sweeping the legs from
under my strength,
You and I, embraced by the surge of the turbulent
waters,
Sweeping around the edges of the stones of the
river,
Driving white into the darkness of the deep pools.
Sing your laughter as the waters curl,
You and I embraced,
Until I hear once more the echoes of the places of
my birth,
Where the waters run between the rocks of the
gorges
As they stand on guard,
Under the scented pines.
You, the swirling torrent of my life,
That I cannot resist,
Hold me among the thousand voices that you
learnt
From the river that learnt from the place where
the eagles fly
And the red deer drink at the darkening.

My love for the land is no longer;
My love is in the sweeping of the waters,
And in you,
Singing the songs of our hearts
Among the surge of the foaming bubbles
On their way to the waiting sea.
You, the swirling torrent of my life
That I cannot resist any longer,
Take me up and hold me!
From the arms of your caring, when the wind
                                    blows strong,.

Never now let me go!
This is my destiny.

SUNLIGHT ON THE SEA

Nothing at all improper
In the way I looked at you,
For I'd heard about you
Years and years ago,
And now,
Watching your face,
Showing me miles and miles of sky
Across that awaited room.
It seemed like a sailor's return
After Atlantic storm,
Catching the first far glimpse
Of the rose-red cliffs of Hoy.

Perhaps we shall never meet
After that yesterday,
But should it be so
I shall never forget
The landfall,
The welcoming home
In the back of those heavenly eyes
So full of unlimited blue.

They told me all of your life
In the miracle flash of time,
Blend of the Moray Firth
And a far Norwegian fjord.
So wherever I go I shall always remember
The wonderful lift that you gave
To that one fine day of my wild mad life,
Strange woman who came so late!

MILTON WITH MEREDYTH

Not what you might have thought –
The two old dears beside the fire
On winter evenings
Reading from *Paradise Lost*.
Nor had it anything to do
With Meredith spelt with an 'i' –
"Lovely are the curves of the white owl sweep-
ing"
Etc., etc.
Nothing to do with cocktail parties either
In high society drawing rooms,
Or drinking port by candlelight.

I was in Venice long ago,
Saw the canals
Clogged up with filth and orange peel
So I thought I understood when Meredyth BDS
Armed to the teeth,
Looking as though she'd earned her soubriquet
'Butcher of Cockermouth' and more,
Announced she wished to clear my blocked
                                    canals.

Relaxed, I waited for the worst,
Not quite prepared for all the awfulness
Of having nappy cleaner squirted up
My fine redundant teeth.

...continues

To be quite fair she told me that
The one before the last
Thought she had poisoned him.
She fixed a pad to keep it in,
I tasted nothing at the time
Thanked her, prepared to pay my bill,
But wasn't even asked –
And left.

It took me full two hundred miles
Thirty miles north of Perth, until the awful truth
Managed to pierce my addled brain.
While arsenic in tiny quantities is good
An overdose is fatal and I also hoped
The patient who had questioned her
Was still alive.
I understood, Milton, I fear,
Is just the same!
So Milton with Meredyth does not mean
The wonder woman, Meredyth Bell and I
Are destined for a cosy fireside chat.

ON BEN ALDER AT NIGHT

Slipped stone beneath my heel;
Echoes in chasms deep below;
Body at strain on vicious ridge
And sharp rocks shine and hill mists flow.

The peaks above
Gashed black upon the brilliant moon:
Iced blood
And every hour the moaning wind
Scoring its music to dispel our mood.
Rhythm beyond all fear of plunging death
No thought of self or sliding boot;
Pure harmony prised back from near despair
The poise from rocks beneath my foot.

FOR SOLVEIG

You came – but much too late,
Setting my fading eyes alight
With echoes of a long forgotten youth.
That was the evening when we met
At Muncaster.
I told you things I do not tell
To other people. My life is past
But just for that one moment
Of a summer night
You opened up once more
The avenues of ebbing time
With sunlit days at peace
In landscapes that I've tried
So hard to keep
Free from the ravages
Of generations who can never understand
The harmony of sun and cloud
Against the backdrop of the fells;
And the garden which is
An essential part of me,
What did it mean;
The fleeting glimpse behind your eyes
Of a Norway that you too
Try to keep safe from all the world's
Uncertain whims. The garden here
Is very beautiful. Some other spring
I long to show it to you and your family
But now my back grows tired

And hands grow weak
With endless pruning of the plants
I treat as wayward children yet.
The work seems pointless now
Without my wife;
With other generations drowned in technology
Who seem unable yet to understand
The countryside needs loving
Even without some scientific explanation;
Nor politicians who clothe our days
Decorating them like Christmas trees
With endless regulations quite irrelevant
To the lives of those who live
More than a mile or two
From Central London.
It needs other people, like you, my sweet
To carry on the fight for a better tomorrow
For the places that we both have loved
And those who follow us.
Soon it will be time for me to go,
Home to the west beyond the Hebrides
To find my own Valhalla,
But right until the end, your smile
Will remain, a constant in my mind,
A perfect memory of that one evening
I shall never forget
Until the end of time.

*(written on the evening when the Nordic Council
came to dinner at Muncaster)*

BLOODY HOUSE!

There is no rest for the wicked
In this heap of stones,
Pink granite and decaying
Freestone architraves.
It's Saturday. The house needs rest,
Like its inhabitants, though as I said
There is – no rest for the wicked!
Saturdays it's usually closed for weddings,
But not today, February 20th,
My sister's birthday, she's seventy seven.
And this obsession with bums on seats
Which seems to possess my wife, my daughter
And my son-in law will kill us all –
For what? What on earth for?
Far more important than the pile of stones
Are the plants in the beautiful garden,
With the loop of the River Esk below
And the timeless views of the valley
With the fells at the top
In their mantle of pure white snow,
Totally independent
Of this bloody heap of stones!

LAGGAN

This is a troubled place
And I, a man of peace,
Seeking a haven in the rocks
Where the water and the wild wind
Cannot break my shelter stone –
Somewhere I can find rest.
People went away to war from this place,
Or to the cities further south,
Not just because of the rapacity of greedy lairds
So much as through sheer economic circumstance.
On the warring tribes who remain,
Seeking for land and their
Justification of each one's separate life,
I have tried to scatter peace
Like the petals of the sweet briars
Under the Corrieyarrick on the evening wind
It is not riches that will satisfy their whims
But only power over each one's own destiny,
And others, whom all see
As equal to themselves.
Such power does not exist, not anywhere.
There can be no security of mind,
Only a mirage from the days of summers past.
Those all too few who have tried hard
To be at ease with what they have

Will always have to watch their dream of peace
Be filched by fighting neighbours.
Peace there can never be –
Only the ultimate dissolution of death,
And yet, I continue to hope –
To strive for a better world
Where enough is enough
And the inborn greed of wanting more
No longer fashionable.

NIGHT AFTER NIGHT

Night after night –
No likely end in sight
To waiting for a finish to our homelessness.
'This year, next year, sometime, never.'
Counting plumstones on my plate at lunch.

Night after night
Of violent storm
Without the comfort of your sleeping limbs
Entwined with mine;
With east wind banging on the window pane,
Only to wake
To days of boring paperwork
Which help me to forget sometimes.

But when the evening comes again,
And the snow blots out the moon,
I wait –
And wonder if the absent hours
Can ever terminate
The awful truth that you're not here,
Beside me, for each minute of the rest of time.

A Whisper of the Wind

You came,
Like a whisper of the spring wind
Out of a long ago
Unexpected and un-awaited
But fresh as the first primrose buds
In the banks along the Birkby road
Beside the river Esk
With the hazel catkins
From my long departed youth
Shaking their pollen
On the evening breeze.
Before too long the geese
Will fly to the north once more,
And soon I shall start my dialogue
With the newly returned swallows
Rebuilding their nests in the eaves
Above the library
When I open the gallery shutters at dawn.
Then perhaps – just perhaps –
If I am lucky with the shake of the dice
We two may meet again.

WITHOUT YOU

My land is nothing without you,
But you are gone. You're never able
To be there,
And I am dying
Of a great sadness.
The Gaelic proverb states:
'Hearing the wheatear on the dyke of holes
I knew my year would not be well.'
The sun is shining
And the hills don't change,
But the land is ill at ease,
And I,
I am dying of a great thirst,
Without you there to share enough
In the beauty
Of my life's evening.
Last week
I heard the wheatear on the dyke
And heard a bell
In some far kirkyard
Close to the island seas,
Calling for me –
Alone,
With you not there!

AT THE WISHING WELL

When I am old
Will you be only memory?
Or will you stand
As you have stood just now
For all the years
Four square beside me
On the battlefield?

Tonight I cannot tell.
I do not sleep.
I know you better
Than you know yourself.
And know your needs.
You know how much I need your love
Until the course of life is run.

I still have many wrongs to right,
And many more campaigns to win,
Although without you now
I'd have no stomach
For the final fight.

So many years ago today
You walked across the threshold of my world.
You gave me hope;
You trusted me and taught me self respect –
Brought music to my silenced mind,
And when tomorrow dawns
I do not want to contemplate
My life alone.

I want you for yourself –
As I want you to want me for myself,
Not some lost memory.
Our tense was always present in the past,
Thus may it always be.

FROM LISMORE

We planted the trees today
In the sight of the sea,
And in the shadow of the seagulls' wings.
It was an act of grace,
Not so graceful as the arc of the white birds' flight
But an act of faith and defiance none the less,
One small atom of dust to fling
In the eyes of the world's destroyers
With their bombs
And their pledge to kill.
It will solve no problems
For a starving world.
Serve no
Material benefit.
But to those who come after it will show
That we had a belief which sustained us.

And so, today, we planted the trees
Underneath the wheeling wings,
With the breeze in our faces,
And in our minds
The thought of the shading leaves
Over the generations to come.

REQUIEM

Beloved One,

    The waves are lapping
    At my clansmen's oars
    And my galley lifts
    On the rising tide.

Soon, soon,

    I shall have to set my sails to the west
    Beyond the April world,
    Learning to leave behind
    The days of our longing.

No Man Can Tell

    Where the winds will take me,
    But this I know –
    And you know too –
    Within my heart your roof tree is.

Wherever You May Be,

You will always be
A part of me
And I of you, for that
Can never be taken away from us.

Pinned to your heart

With pride you wear
The emblem of my clan,
And in your head
The thought of the blue, and the green,
And the red, and the brown of my tartan,
Which you can never wear again,
Except in my mind's eye.

But now the boat

Is waiting on the tide
And I must go.

IN THE PEERS LOBBY, HOUSE OF LORDS

Guide dog in the Peers Lobby;
Lovely Northern Irish girl from the police
Checking the suitors as they come and go;
Peers and peeresses I know
From more than thirty years ago,
Now with thickened waists
And balding pates, amid
An air of mild gentility.
We wait – wondering how long
The genteel club can last.

THE DARK MILE

I cannot bear the din
Of all the heavy footed people over head.
They called it grave and grave it is.
A sleepless misery at being apart
From separated friends.
They think I'm deaf, the children's children,
When all I want to do
Is sleep, and sleep, until some morrow
Which may never come, so let me be!
Long, long ago I lived and loved
Within a wider world full of the many
People who have sheltered me on whose behalf
I battled with authorities who never learnt
To comprehend their modest needs;
Who interfered with endless niggles
Quite unnecessary, in everybody's private lives
But now they'll soon forget me, I suppose,
Both friend and foe alike,
And I must moulder in the ghastly silent soil
Which gave me a living in the sunlit days,
Without the need of intervention
From politics or science based in offices,
Where civil servants hate the non-conformist zeal
Of those like me, opposed to them.
I hate myself for hating them,
But hate still more the thought
Of being irrelevant, so now
I miss the music of my one time life

...continues

Hoping the world may end
Quite soon, but not before
I hear the calling of the greylag geese
Going north across the moon again
And the sound of young children
In the hall below my tower
Those, and the cadence of your dear sweet voice
Within my ear at night;
And the call of the curlew
Silent too long in the fields across the valley
As dawn spreads red across the waiting hills,
Those are the sounds of the resurrection
And the call for battle again.
Take up the claymore one more time
I think my sword is needed still!

FOR THE PEOPLE OF THE KHOLKHOZ
OF THE RED BANNER

You have taken us
Who were strangers only yesterday
Into your hearts.
You have given us the feeling for your lands
And your love for your cattle
Which we can so easily understand.
In two short days
You have handed us so much
Of your kindness
That when we have gone away
To our own homes
We shall never forget
All the beauty we have seen.
Watching the sun and the moon
Rise and go down
Across the wide Siberian lands;
And if we should ever be given the great privilege
Of an invitation to return
We would ask that it should be
At a time of year
When we can plant a tree,
So that when we must leave again
We will have the thought,
Always in our minds,
Of the little birds in its branches
And the shade of its leaves
Over the children of the children
Who met us yesterday

...continues

In the kindergarten of your kholkhoz
Too soon
Shall we go away to our own houses
And our own hills
But our hearts will always be full
Of your people;
And when we watch the moon rise
Over our fields again
We shall know
It is the same moon
Which shines on us
And upon you. We shall shed a tear
Because of the great distance
Which keeps us apart.

I learnt philosophy, once long ago,
But somewhere I have lost myself, I know.
Relationship with God is bad,
Allah has damned me, too;
The eye of Buddha has focussed upon my fallen
                                    thoughts,
Standing upon that cussed middle moon.

As boys
We went to College Chapel every day.
Sung hymns, were roused
By anthems spiralling
Up the stone pillars to the massive roof
While the Germans dropped their bombs on London.

The names of the OEs who had
Been killed that week
Were read out every Saturday night,
People we knew, had sat beside.
Life seemed an heroic struggle.

As boys, we fought each other; translated
Local papers into Latin verse:
Read Virgil, Homer, and Horace.
A thin veneer of culture spread
On young barbaric minds.

We learnt our nation's history, since rewritten.
Now we are told

...continues

We learnt it badly and that those who died
In far off places, in the nineteenth century
Were only cads.

We went to universities and learnt free thought.
And God, too, was taken away.
At 21,
The first moon lost.

As to the hereafter...
Now and then, I found a balance
In what I thought about the hills,
And the true life
Of the people who lived in them,
And their caring, and their kindliness.

In a way, I suppose, it was no more
Than one fresh God I found.
But when the winter came
And snowflakes used to lay themselves among the
                                        pines,
When the first whoopers landed on the loch
Beside the house
I used to find some consolation in the old beliefs.
I knew, or seemed to know...
                        one day, one year,
When spring returned;
When arrowheads of geese flew back across the
                                        Arctic hills,
The wild white swans would carry home my soul
Over the mountains and across the Island seas

To Tir-nan-Og.
At that time I found harmony
Within the moon of After Life.
A place where the power of our physcial pain
would break,
The tiredness fade.

For years I herded sheep.
And killed the deer,
And knew the mountain people's homes.
I followed stags into their desolate holy places
Among the wind, and the rocks, and the diamond
waters;
But now I have lost all of my belief,
Can only stand,
Self in the middle moon.
Alone,
Wondering why.
Life only a lament for lost simplicity
In an ugly world, and I, too old,
To seek its meaning here
At Muncaster.

Yet here I have to be,
Anchored within the circle of the Middle Moon.
All that are left
Are the moons which stand
For Work
And Love... ...
And all my life
Which stands for you.

Death Throes of an Old World

Summer gone.
No swallows now
Swinging around the cart shed eaves
At Gallovie.
Silent the leafless aspens in
These winter days.
Last August month I watched them from my bed
At dawn, the rustles of the south west wind
Among the brilliant leaves, while far
Out on the hill ring ouzels and dippers
Flitter among the stones of the Moy burn.
And the falling leaves from the blood red rowans
Dropping earlier and earlier as the years
Run past.
Out of these windows from the drawing room
Looking west tonight
I watch
The Window of Corrarder lit
By the moonlight on the snow,
Places I herded Blackface sheep
Those nine and forty years ago,
Corrie Chrannaig and the Corrie of the Lost
Meall Ghorlaig and Meall Damh,
The hill of the deer
Where the last clan battle was fought
MacPhersons and MacDonalds
Who had stolen their cattle
And were driving them back to Lochaber.
No whiteness now below.

You wouldn't believe
My photographs of snow, drifted level
With the tops of the sitting room windows
At Aberarder Farm in '55.
Then I was hard and lean,
Away to the hill
In my kilt with my dogs, my tartan plaid
Around my shoulders. There were
Chilbains on my knees as I ploughed the field
For Murdie's potatoes that spring.
At lambing time,
After a bowl of porridge we left for the hill
In the almost dark to be back at the house
By nine for breakfast and the milking of the cow,
Head wonderfully warm on the animal's flank
And the soothing sound of milk in the bucket.
Fit and happy, we returned to the hill
At afternoon. On the nineteenth of May
There were six inches of snow
And a north west gale driving it like sand
Stinging our faces as we trampled tracks
For sheep herding them to shelter
Among the birches, reuniting ewes with lambs
Separated by swollen burns.
In summer to the gathering at 3am.
To meet the neighbouring shepherds at the march
And drive the ribbons of sheep
From the faraway hillsides
Down to the fank in the cool of the day,

...*continues*

For the handlings, and I
Was only an ignorant youth of 25
Taught by my dogs and Neil Usher,
And Duncan MacNaughton, the head shepherd
Who had a pet fox. Once
A hole had to be dug for a Highland cow
Which died. At nights
I lay on my bed in the bothy
Reading books, flickering flame of the fire in the
grate
Fuelled by coal from the woodshed
Where the cat had a litter of half wild kittens
Which spat. Today, broken in spirit
By pain in my back, I seem to be going
Into an endless tomorrow of nothingness.
No leaves now on the aspens and most
Of the friends who taught me the wisdoms of life
Have gone. What on earth was it all about?
But suddenly – into this sad deserted land –
You came, brightness and light
Into my winter countryside.

REMINDER OF THE GRAIL

On a night in the middle of all this winter
You came as a faltering flame
Into the ice-filled caverns
Of a silent sadness.
You came as a reminder
Of exultations of larks in the June skies
And sunlight on the span of eagles' wings
You came as a reminder
Of resin rising in the silent trees
And in the bursting blue of the milkwort buds
In the mountain pastures.

And when you came
I knew that spring would come,
Knew we should travel for a little time
Along the winding way
In our search for the grail
Certain sure that we shall never find it,
Yet comforted by the closeness
Of a seeking together
On the endless road

GRACE À DIEU

Out today at dawn
With the morning's earlier light
And the tide flooding
And the sound of geese in the sky
Above the marsh, talking of leaving
For the breeding grounds.
I thought of you
And sensed the swelling buds
Ready to break,
And the feeling in the air that soon,
Quite soon, the sound of whaups
And oyster catchers
Flying across the moon
Would echo through the valley night,
Once more.
"Spring will be soon again this year"
The robins told me as I walked
Along the drive, the way it came
Early for me, with you
Breaking through a closed door
Into my unsuspecting life
Those so many months ago,
Lighting dark chasms of nothingness
With a love I long thought dead.

In the Pentland Hills, 1952

I watched a bumble bee
Thrusting its head
Into the throat
Of a harebell flower
And knew exactly how it felt
That summer day
Intoxicated with the nectar
Drunk and a little insane
From what it found –
As I found you
Just yesterday and knew
The touching of your loving tongue
Come home at last
To rest on mine.

Oh! God –
The cry comes all too easily
From unbelievers' mouths –
But Oh! Dear God
What must we do
To quiet our purgatory
And find each other
In the silent night.
You're there, I'm here,
Knowing too well
The joys we almost touch,
Adam and Eve,
The apples just, but only just
Beyond our reach.
So "God" we cry,
Not going to church
But brought up well enough
To say
Our paternosters under Sunday skies,
Not knowing when, or even if
We shall escape to happiness
Finding our unity in time
Before we die.
So "God"! we cry again
Hoping a little
That the future can repay
For all the agony
Of life apart.

I'M ALWAYS THERE

It hurts me that I cannot give
The one thing that you really need –
A place to rest,
To call your own.

I cannot give you ease,
Or peace of mind,
Or somewhere quiet to lay your head at night.
I can give none of these.

I know you're frightened if I put a foot
Within the circle of the little limbo which
You made yourself;
Frightened
That you will give too much,
And take too much
That might be torn away.
Breaching your circle's frail security.

All I can do
Is wait in patience in the wings,
Saying a little prayer from time to time,
And stay still long enough to let you know
You're not alone.
I'm always there.

THE WIND IN SEPTEMBER TREES

The wind is rushing through September trees,
Cries you, and you, and you.
I cannot find you anywhere
Among the draughty corridors,
Nor in the garden woods;
But only here
Among the papers on my office desk
Is peace – and you!

The waves are breaking on the autumn sands.
And cry come back, come back,
But winter lies in front of us,
With you, so many distant miles,
Among the mountains far away.
That all the time your absence is unhappiness.

And yet, for all the wind,
For all the streaming clouds across the moon,
I know deep down
That spring will come again for you and me,
Because of you, I live and breathe,
And when I reach out through the tiresome night
Before I sleep,
Your arms surround me, and your touch brings
                                                    hope
Of spring,
And resin rising in the ancient trees.

At Evening

Beloved one
       The waves are lapping
       At my clansmen's oars
       And my galley lifts
       On the rising tide.

Soon, Soon
       I shall have to set my sails to the west
       Beyond the winter world
       Learning to leave behind
       The days of our longing

No man can tell
       Where the winds will take me
       But this I know –
       And you know too –
       Within my heart
       Your roof tree is

Wherever you may be
       You will always be
       A part of me
       And I of you, for that
       Can never be taken
       Away from us.

...continues

Pinned to your heart
       With pride you wear
       The emblem of my clan
       And in your head
       The thought of the blue and the green
       And the red and the brown
       Of my tartan
       Which you can never wear again
       Except in my mind's eye.

But now the boat
       Is waiting on the tide
       And I must go.